# BUFFALO SABRES

BY DAVID J. CLARKE

Book design by Maggie Villaume
Cover design by Maggie Villaume

Photographs ©: Scott Kane/AP Images, cover; Jeffrey T. Barnes/AP Images, 4–5, 27; Joshua Bessex/AP Images, 7, 8; AP Images, 10–11, 13; Shutterstock Images, 15; Rusty Kennedy/AP Images, 16–17; Don Heupel/AP Images, 19; Gene Puskar/AP Images, 21; David Duprey/AP Images, 22–23; Karl Deblaker/AP Images, 24–25; Bill Kostroun/AP Images, 28

Press Box Books, an imprint of Press Room Editions.

**ISBN**
978-1-63494-673-5 (library bound)
978-1-63494-697-1 (paperback)
978-1-63494-743-5 (epub)
978-1-63494-721-3 (hosted ebook)

**Library of Congress Control Number: 2022948150**

Distributed by North Star Editions, Inc.
2297 Waters Drive
Mendota Heights, MN 55120
www.northstareditions.com

Printed in the United States of America
Mankato, MN
082023

## ABOUT THE AUTHOR

David J. Clarke is a freelance sportswriter. Originally from Helena, Montana, he now lives in Savannah, Georgia, with his golden retriever, Gus.

# TABLE OF
# CONTENTS

**1**

Owen Power
warms up
before his first
home game in
April 2022.

# THE POWER HOUR

The Buffalo Sabres struggled a lot in the 2010s. The 2020–21 season was no different. They finished with the worst record in the National Hockey League (NHL). There was a silver lining, though. All that losing earned them the top pick in the NHL Draft. The Sabres selected promising defenseman Owen Power. The strong Canadian looked like he could be a force.

However, the Sabres wouldn't find out right away. Top draft picks often jump straight into the NHL. But Power stayed at the University of Michigan for the 2021–22 season. There he helped lead the Wolverines to a strong season. The hype kept building in Buffalo.

Finally, on April 8, 2022, Power signed with Buffalo. There were only 10 games remaining in the Sabres' season. Once again, they were set to miss the playoffs. But fans still came out to see what the young defenseman could do.

Power helped the Sabres right away. He had a goal and an assist in his first seven games. And Buffalo went 5–2 during that stretch. But the Sabres looked

Owen Power carries the puck against the Chicago Blackhawks on the final day of the 2021–22 season.

like they were headed for a loss on the final day of the season. They trailed the Chicago Blackhawks 2–1 with just over five minutes left.

Power finished with two goals and one assist in his eight NHL games in 2021–22.

Power helped keep the puck in the offensive zone. Several players whacked at it. The puck eventually bounced back to the big defenseman. Power had the puck on his backhand. He switched to his forehand and got in position to shoot. Then he fired a quick wrist shot that fooled the goaltender. The puck settled in the back of the net to tie the game.

Buffalo eventually won in overtime to finish the season strong. And with young stars like Power coming back again, the future looked bright.

## OLYMPIC OWEN

Power was born in Mississauga, Ontario. He represented his home country at the 2022 Olympics in Beijing, China. He recorded one assist in five games. However, Sweden knocked out Canada in the quarterfinals.

**2**

Gilbert Perreault
recorded
1,326 points in
1,191 career
games for
the Sabres.

# BUILDING IN BUFFALO

The year 1970 was an exciting one in Buffalo, New York. The Buffalo Bills joined the National Football League. The Buffalo Braves were one of three new teams to join the National Basketball Association. And the Buffalo Sabres were one of two new NHL teams. The expansion team struck gold right away. The Sabres selected Gilbert Perreault with their first draft pick. The playmaking center was the team's first star.

A year later he was joined on a line by Rick Martin and René Robert. All three were from the French-speaking Canadian province of Quebec. The line was nicknamed the "French Connection" after a popular 1971 movie.

The French Connection led the Sabres to the playoffs in 1972–73. But they lost in the first round to the Montreal Canadiens.

## SABRE DANCE

Buffalo selected the Sabres nickname through a fan contest. Team owner Seymour Knox liked it. He noted that a sabre is a sword that is good both offensively and defensively. Some of the other options weren't as inspiring. The Sabres beat out names like the Mugwumps, the Buzzing Bees, and the Flying Zeppelins.

René Robert tallied a career-high 100 points in 1974–75, helping the Sabres make a run to the Stanley Cup Final.

Two years later, Buffalo got a rematch with Montreal in the semifinals. The Sabres won the series 4–2 to reach their first Stanley Cup Final.

Buffalo matched up with the Philadelphia Flyers in the 1975 Final. The series featured one of the strangest hockey games ever played. Philadelphia won the first two games at home. Game 3 was played on a hot, humid night in Buffalo. The steamy air outside mixed with the cold air of the rink. The result was a bank of fog throughout the arena. It made the game hard to see for fans and players. There was also a bat that flew around the rink. It got close to Sabres center Jim Lorentz during a faceoff. Lorentz swung his stick at the bat and killed the animal.

The exciting play on the ice soon added to the legend of that game.

The Sabres put up a statue of the French Connection line outside of the team's home arena in 2012.

Buffalo rallied three times to force overtime. Robert ended it on a slap shot through the fog. Buffalo won Game 4 also. But the Flyers shut down the French Connection and took the series in six games.

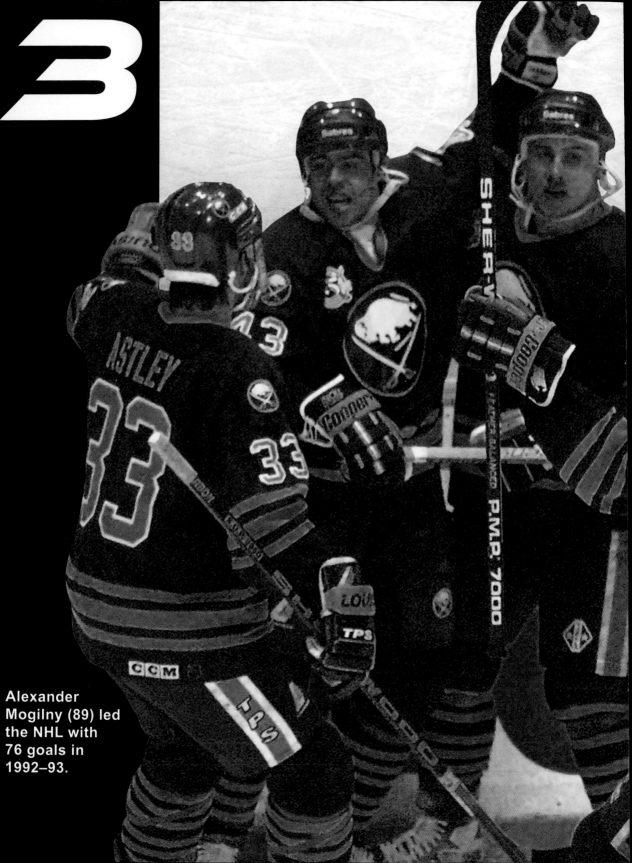

**3**

Alexander Mogilny (89) led the NHL with 76 goals in 1992–93.

# IN THE CREASE

**T**he Sabres remained a playoff team for most of the next two decades. A big reason why was the play of Gilbert Perreault. The other two French Connection forwards were gone by the early 1980s. But Perreault stayed until his retirement in 1986. He never won a championship. But he left holding every major offensive record for Buffalo.

The Sabres found new stars after Perreault's retirement. Forward Alexander Mogilny joined Buffalo in 1989. Mogilny was joined by center Dale Hawerchuk a year later. Center Pat LaFontaine arrived in 1991. The trio made Buffalo an offensive force in the 1990s.

Keeping pucks out of the net was Dominik Hašek. The skinny goaltender was incredibly athletic. Hašek joined

## RICK JEANNERET

Sabres fans heard a familiar voice on television and radio for 51 years. Rick Jeanneret joined the team for the 1971–72 season. His energetic style led to many memorable calls. One of his most famous came in a 1993 playoff game. Enforcer Brad May scored an overtime goal to beat the Boston Bruins. Jeanneret yelled out "May Day!" over and over after the goal. The popular announcer retired after the 2021–22 season.

Buffalo coach Lindy Ruff raises his arms in celebration after the Sabres advanced to the conference finals in 1999.

the Sabres in 1992. He eventually won six Vezina Trophies as the league's best netminder.

Hašek also led the Sabres back to the Stanley Cup Final in 1999. There they met the Dallas Stars. Once again, the series featured a memorable overtime game. Dallas led the series 3–2 heading into Game 6 in Buffalo. The Sabres needed a win to stay alive. Buffalo forward Stu Barnes scored with just over a minute left in the second period. That tied the game 1–1. From that point on, Hašek and Dallas goalie Ed Belfour stopped every shot. The game eventually went into a third overtime.

Hašek made a tough save late in the third overtime. But Dallas forward Brett Hull scored off the rebound. Replays showed that Hull's left skate was in the goalie's crease. It was against the rules for skaters to be standing in the crease. To this day, Buffalo fans believe the goal

Brett Hull's left skate crept into the crease before his game-winning goal in the 1999 Stanley Cup Final.

should not have counted. But the play

stood. And Buffalo lost the series.

# DOMINIK HAŠEK

Dominik Hašek started his career as a backup goalie for the Chicago Blackhawks. The Sabres traded for him in 1992. The Czech goalie was 28 years old at the time. But he was about to become a huge star. Hašek won his first Vezina Trophy a year later. He then won the award in four of the next five years. In 1997 and 1998, Hašek won both the Vezina and the Hart Memorial Trophy. The Hart is given to the best player in the league. No goalie had ever won it twice.

Hašek never won a Stanley Cup with the Sabres. But his best years came during his nine seasons with the team. When he retired at age 43 in 2008, he had a .922 save percentage. That was the highest in NHL history. It was no wonder fans called him the "Dominator."

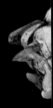

Dominik Hašek led the league in save percentage
for six straight seasons from 1993–94
to 1998–99 while playing with Buffalo

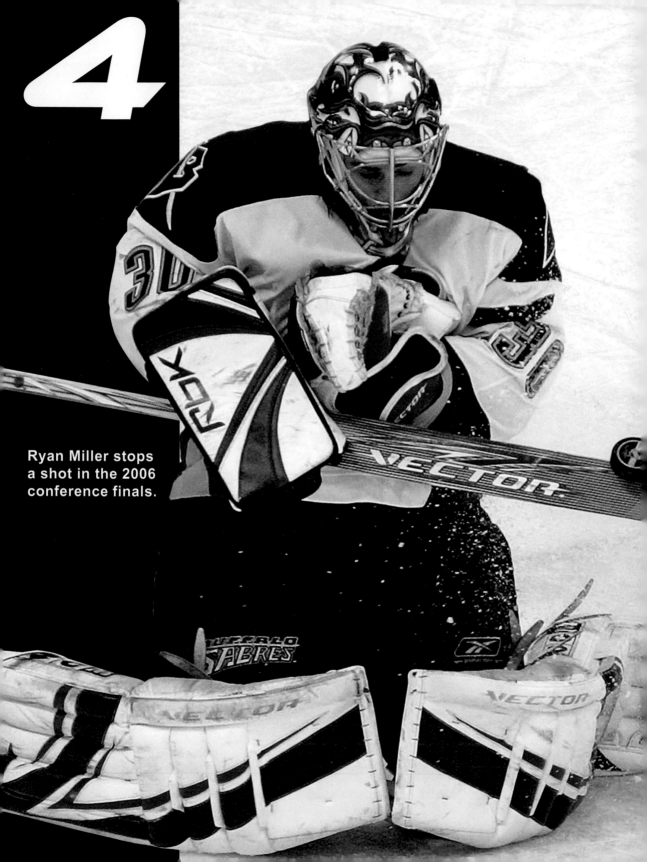

**4**

Ryan Miller stops a shot in the 2006 conference finals.

# RATTLING SABRES

**T**hings got much worse for the Sabres after their run to the 1999 Stanley Cup Final. The team ran out of money. Stars like Dominik Hašek were traded. Starting in 2001–02, Buffalo missed the playoffs for three straight years.

That ended in a big way in 2005–06. The Sabres won 52 games. That was a new team record. Slick forwards like Daniel Brière, Tim Connolly, and

Thomas Vanek paced the offense. In goal was another standout, Ryan Miller.

The Sabres reached the conference finals that season. They were eliminated in seven games by the Carolina Hurricanes. But the next year Buffalo was just as good. The Sabres started the season 10–0. They went on to set a new team record with 53 wins. But another playoff run was stopped in the conference finals. This time the Ottawa Senators beat Buffalo in five games.

All of that success came under head coach Lindy Ruff. But the Sabres began to fall off and eventually missed the playoffs. Midway through the 2012–13 season, Ruff was fired.

Jack Eichel tallied 355 points in six seasons with Buffalo.

Buffalo eventually earned the second pick in the 2015 draft. The team used it on promising center Jack Eichel. He looked like the superstar the Sabres could build

Tage Thompson takes a shot against the New Jersey Devils in an April 2022 game.

around. Eichel put up good numbers for six seasons. But the team missed the playoffs every year.

Eichel was eventually traded away in November 2021. Buffalo moved forward with a new set of young stars. Defensemen Rasmus Dahlin and rookie Owen Power formed a strong blue line partnership. And forward Tage Thompson scored 38 goals in the 2021–22 season. The future was once again looking up in Buffalo.

## THE LONG WAIT

The Sabres missed the playoffs after the 2021–22 season. It was their 11th straight year out of the postseason. That was the longest playoff drought in NHL history. It's not the only ugly streak for Buffalo. The Sabres and the Vancouver Canucks have both been playing since 1970. As of 2022, neither had won the Stanley Cup. No NHL teams had been playing longer without winning a title.

# • BUFFALO SABRES
# QUICK STATS

**TEAM HISTORY:** Buffalo Sabres (1970– )

**STANLEY CUP CHAMPIONSHIPS:** 0

**KEY COACHES:**

- Floyd Smith (1972, 1974–77): 143 wins, 62 losses, 36 ties

- Scotty Bowman (1980–86): 210 wins, 134 losses, 60 ties

- Lindy Ruff (1997–2013): 571 wins, 432 losses, 78 ties, 84 overtime losses

**HOME ARENA:** KeyBank Center (Buffalo, NY)

**MOST CAREER POINTS:** Gilbert Perreault (1,326)

**MOST CAREER GOALS:** Gilbert Perreault (512)

**MOST CAREER ASSISTS:** Gilbert Perreault (814)

**MOST CAREER SHUTOUTS:** Dominik Hašek (55)

*Stats are accurate through the 2021–22 season.*

# GLOSSARY

**CREASE**
The painted area in front of each goal.

**DRAFT**
An event that allows teams to choose new players coming into the league.

**ENFORCER**
A hockey player who is mostly known for physical play and protecting teammates.

**EXPANSION TEAM**
A new team added to a professional sports league.

**OVERTIME**
One or more extra periods played after regulation if a game is still tied.

**REBOUND**
When the goalie makes a save, but the puck goes back into play.

**ZONE**
One of three areas on a hockey rink that are separated by blue lines.

# • TO LEARN
# MORE

## BOOKS

Berglund, Bruce. *Big-Time Hockey Records*. North Mankato, MN: Capstone Press, 2022.

Davidson, B. Keith. *NHL*. New York: Crabtree Publishing, 2022.

Doeden, Matt. *G.O.A.T. Hockey Teams*. Minneapolis: Lerner Publications, 2021.

## MORE INFORMATION

To learn more about the Buffalo Sabres, go to **pressboxbooks.com/AllAccess**.

These links are routinely monitored and updated to provide the most current information available.

## INDEX